POSTCARD HISTORY SERIES

Starved Rock
State Park

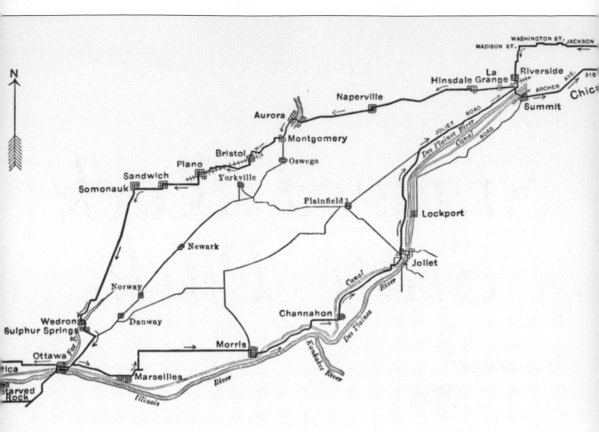

FOLLOW THE HARD ROAD TO STARVED ROCK, 1914. Follow this map for a delightful weekend automobile trip from Chicago to Starved Rock. According to a souvenir edition of *Starved Rock Beautiful (Illinois State Park)*, published by the Ottawa Printing Company in 1914, "Motorists from Chicago go out to the end of Washington Boulevard and follow the well marked trail all the way to the Park." Chicagoans could also take the Chicago, Ottawa and Peoria Railway.

On the front cover: **STARVED ROCK, AN ILLINOIS STATE PARK, c. 1907–1915.** Towering high above the Illinois River between Ottawa and LaSalle is the huge bulk of Starved Rock. Starved Rock State Park is located 95 miles southwest of Chicago. The 2,630 acres of the park today include 18 sandstone canyons and 16 miles of well-marked hiking trails. Many scenic views, including bluffs, canyons, the river, and wildlife, are found throughout the park. Hiking, boating, camping, fishing, and picnicking are just some of the activities enjoyed by visitors. (Author's collection.)

On the back cover: **LASALLE CANYON WATERFALL, 1922.** For a unique experience, hikers can walk behind the waterfall in LaSalle Canyon, one of the most beautiful in the park. (Author's collection.)

Starved Rock State Park

Nancy Hill Barta

ARCADIA
PUBLISHING

Published by Arcadia Publishing
Charleston SC, Chicago IL, Portsmouth NH, San Francisco CA

Printed in the United States of America

Library of Congress Catalog Card Number: 2007923785

For all general information contact Arcadia Publishing at:
Telephone 843-853-2070
Fax 843-853-0044
E-mail sales@arcadiapublishing.com
For customer service and orders:
Toll-Free 1-888-313-2665

Visit us on the Internet at www.arcadiapublishing.com

CONTENTS

ACKNOWLEDGMENTS

My sincere thanks and appreciation go to my mother, Lois Hill, a retired teacher who "red-penciled" my work. I give my thanks and appreciation to my husband, Mike, for his technical support in the proper scanning of postcards and for putting up with my collecting "habits." I would also like to thank my brother, Harold, and my children, Lyndsey and Jaerod, for their support and encouragement.

Louis Joliet and Fr. Jacques Marquette were not only perhaps the first Europeans to see Starved Rock, but thanks to them, and others who followed, we have some knowledge of what the Starved Rock area and even the world was like in 1673 through their journals. These written reminders as well as stories that have been passed down through the years help us visualize a life that is so much different than life is today.

My thanks also go to early photographers who captured for us these long gone and long forgotten images. From the mid-1800s, when the first postcards were made, until now, these cards have offered a treasure trove of fascinating stories, photographs, memories, information, and history.

Thanks should also be given to the local residents who had the vision of developing the Starved Rock area for a park and to the residents of Illinois for making it happen. What a gift!

INTRODUCTION

It has been great fun for me to bring this book to you. Having lived most of my life in the Starved Rock area, I want to let others know of the history, the natural beauty, and the serene surroundings that we in the area have long treasured. My love for Starved Rock as well as collecting has led me to write this book and to share my collection of postcards with others.

As you turn the pages, you will discover how little Starved Rock has changed over the years. The rock formations left by glaciers more than 4,000 years ago and the Illinois River had a great impact on early development. Native Americans, French missionaries and explorers, and pioneers have traveled through the woods, canoed the river, crossed the prairie, climbed the rocks, hiked the canyons, and forded the streams. The fertile soils, the abundant wildlife, and the resources of the river provided a rich life for these early inhabitants.

The grand village of the Kaskaskia and the surrounding Illinois River valley area was the site of the greatest Native American encampment ever found in one area in the continental United States. The grand village of the Kaskaskia, or LaVantum as it was called by the Native Americans, was directly across the river from Starved Rock. Native American lore is intertwined with how Starved Rock got its name. Legend has it that Chief Pontiac of the Ottawa tribe was killed by an Illiniwek at a tribal council. A battle began. The Illiniwek sought refuge on the top of the rock, and the Ottawa surrounded the rock. The Illiniwek eventually died from starvation. From then on the rock was known as Starved Rock.

Louis Joliet and Fr. Jacques Marquette were the first white men to set eyes on the rock in 1673. In 1675, they returned to the area, and Marquette founded the Mission of the Immaculate Conception, the first Christian mission in Illinois, at the Kaskaskia Indian village. These two men also provided us with the first recorded history of Illinois and the Midwest through their journals. Later Fr. Louis Hennepin made the first discovery of coal in the New World along the river.

The next men to see the rock were the greatest of all French explorers, René-Robert Cavelier, Sieur de LaSalle, and his companion Henri de Tonti. LaSalle authorized Tonti to build Fort St. Louis on the rock overlooking the Illinois River. This fort became the center of French influence and power and formed a nucleus for the first white settlement in Illinois.

Other notable people followed, including Abraham Lincoln, who may have passed through this area and stayed at the Sulphur Springs Hotel or Half-Way House as he traveled the Illinois circuit. Jenny Lind, the "Swedish Nightingale," who was brought to America by P. T. Barnum, may have sung at the Sulphur Springs Hotel located across the river from the rock.

Starved Rock became a popular summer resort in the 1890s. Some of the guests arrived at the Starved Rock Hotel by boat after being picked up at the depot in Utica. Gloria Swanson stayed at the hotel while working on a film, and Benny Goodman, Guy Lombardo, and Duke Ellington entertained guests with their unforgettable music.

Many popular destinations of the time had romantic tragedies associated with them. The story of Lover's Leap at Starved Rock is tragic. Two young lovers were forbidden to marry by the chief of their tribes. Rather than live without one another, they joined hands and leapt together from the rock to the turbulent waters of the Illinois River below.

The Starved Rock Lock and Dam, directly across the river from the rock, was built as part of the Illinois Waterway Project to provide a permanent nine-foot-deep navigable channel between the Great Lakes and the Mississippi River. During World War II, more than 1,200 war vessels passed through the locks at Starved Rock.

Starved Rock Lodge, built in part by the Civilian Conservation Corps in the 1930s, is one of the finest park lodges in the Midwest. The corps was developed by Pres. Franklin Delano Roosevelt as part of the New Deal program. During the Great Depression, many men were without work, and this program not only helped support families and the economy, but it also helped build and improve many parks and historic sites. The Civilian Conservation Corps companies at Starved Rock State Park built cabins and shelters, developed trails, built the fireplace and furnishings in the lodge, and much more.

Starved Rock is one of the highest elevations in Illinois, towering over 100 feet above the Illinois River. The park, as well as Starved Rock Lodge and the lock and dam, is listed on the National Register of Historic Places.

Beautiful wildflowers, trees, bridges, trails, wildlife, waterfalls, and canyons are just some of the sights a visitor to the park can enjoy. Other activities include picnicking, boating, fishing, hunting, hiking, and much more.

The park is located 95 miles southwest of Chicago between Ottawa and LaSalle. This popular Illinois state park covers approximately 2,630 acres, including 18 canyons. The State of Illinois purchased the original 280 acres in 1911 for $146,000. Today the park is enjoyed by millions of visitors each year.

Through postcards of the park, including the rock, the canyons, the waterfalls, the hotel and lodge, the Illinois River, Lover's Leap, the lock and dam, and much more, one will gain a better appreciation for the jewel of LaSalle County—Starved Rock State Park.

One

THE ROCK
AND ITS LEGEND

Starved Rock, Height 158 ft., in New State Park, near Ottawa and La Salle, Ill.

STARVED ROCK NEAR UTICA, 1907–1915. Starved Rock is among the highest elevations in Illinois, rising over 100 feet. It is a gray, cylindrical pillar of St. Peter sandstone with a perpendicular wall overlooking the Illinois River. St. Peter sandstone is an Ordovician formation that spans north and south from Minnesota to Missouri and east and west from Illinois into Nebraska and South Dakota. The sandstone varies in color from gray or brown to white, yellow, and even red. It is almost pure quartz and is used for making glass, building stones, as an abrasive, and as molding sand. Large tonnages of St. Peter sandstone are mined in LaSalle County. The sandstone is named after the St. Peter River in Minnesota where it was first identified.

STARVED ROCK STATE PARK, c. 1907–1915. Prehistoric Native Americans as early as 8000 BC, including Hopewelian, Woodland, and Mississippian cultures, thrived in the Illinois valley. The abundance of wildlife, the Illinois River, and rich fertile soils made for an ideal home. Tribes hunted buffalo and wild game and caught fish in the river. The river also provided easy transportation. Large crops of corn, pumpkins, and beans were grown in the fertile bottomlands.

STARVED ROCK, c. 1907–1915. Approximately 5,000 to 7,000 Kaskaskias, a subtribe of the Illiniwek, lived in a village along the north bank of the Illinois River across from Starved Rock. This grand village of the Kaskaskia, or LaVantum as it was called by the Native Americans, grew until 460 cabins were known to have existed.

STARVED ROCK AND THE SURROUNDING ILLINOIS RIVER VALLEY, C. 1907–1915. The Starved Rock and the Illinois River valley area was the site of the greatest Native American encampment ever found in one area in the continental United States. In 1800, the U.S. commissioners of Indian Affairs estimated 30,000 Native Americans were living in Illinois, and approximately three-fifths were living along the Illinois River.

LOOKING EAST TO STARVED ROCK, C. 1907–1915. Native American tribes that lived in the Starved Rock area were the Iroquois, the Fox, the Sauk, the Potawatomi, the Ottawa, the Chippewa, the Winnebago, the Kickapoo, and the Illiniwek. The Illiniwek were also referred to as the Illinois and the Illini tribes. The Native American impact on the region was so great that it led to the State of Illinois naming itself for the Illiniwek tribe, which means "tribe of superior men."

STARVED ROCK IN LaSALLE COUNTY, C. 1907–1913. The first white men to see the rock were Louis Joliet and Fr. Jacques Marquette, who erected a cross on the summit of the rock in the name of France and the church. They had traveled from Montreal to Arkansas on their way up the Illinois River from the Mississippi River in 1673. Native Americans had told them of a shorter route back to the Great Lakes. In taking this different route they happened upon the principal village of the Illiniwek, Kaskaskia. Chief Casogoac, chief of the Illiniwek, treated Marquette and Joliet kindly, but they continued paddling up the river in their birch bark canoes to return to their mission in Michigan. The sail on each canoe had a French coat of arms, a pipe of peace, and a cross for Christianity painted on it.

STARVED ROCK NEAR OTTAWA, c. 1906–1915. Joliet and Marquette returned to the Illinois valley area in 1675. They named Starved Rock the Rock of St. Louis. The Illiniwek prepared a huge feast of fish, bison, cornmeal, and dog in their honor. The dog meat was not relished by the explorers, but it was considered a delicacy by their Native American hosts. The phrase "putting on the dog" is believed to have begun from the Illiniwek tribes. The Illiniwek hand-fed Marquette and Joliet from bark trays filled with food. Marquette later wrote in his journal that he thought the best Native American food was wild rice mixed with buffalo fat. The first recorded history of Illinois and the Midwest was told through journals of the early missionaries and explorers from the Starved Rock area.

STARVED ROCK ON THE ILLINOIS RIVER, C. 1907–1915. Jesuit Fr. Jacques Marquette was known as "Père," the French word for *father.* Marquette quickly learned many Native American tongues and dialects, which gained him much respect and aided his dream to spread Christianity among the Native Americans. In 1675, Marquette founded the Mission of the Immaculate Conception at the Kaskaskia village, where he celebrated Easter mass on April 14 with over 5,000 Native Americans in attendance. The Kaskaskia village extended from the present site of Utica to Buffalo Rock along the Illinois River. The cabins of the Illiniwek looked like long arbors and were covered with rushes. Wind, snow, or rain never penetrated these cabins. Eight to ten families lived in one cabin, and each cabin had four to five fires to keep them warm and cook their food.

Starved Rock, 30 years ago; formerly Fort St. Louis, discovered by Marquette and Jolliet in 1673, fortified by Tonti and De la Salle in 1682, abandoned in 1702, and is the first white settlement in the Mississippi Valley. Highest elevation in Illinois, now famous summer resort near Ottawa, Utica, La Salle and Peru, Ill.

Starved Rock State Park,
near Ottawa, Utica and
La Salle, Ill.—1

STARVED ROCK FROM THE RIVER AND FROM LOVER'S LEAP, C. 1915–1930. Over 200 years later, on October 14, 1951, at St. Mary's Church in Utica, a granite memorial to honor Fr. Jacques Marquette was dedicated and placed at the site. A small bag of sand from Marquette's grave was placed in the center of the concrete foundation. Earlier that day a mass was celebrated at the base of Starved Rock just as Marquette had done many years earlier. The Mission of the Immaculate Conception was Illinois's first Christian mission. This mission near Starved Rock did not have the opportunity to flourish before Marquette's death. He was forced to return to his mission in St. Ignace, Michigan, due to ill health. He died at age 38 en route to the mission and is buried at the site of the St. Ignace Mission Chapel.

THE VIEW FROM THE SUMMIT OF STARVED ROCK, C. 1915–1930. After Fr. Jacques Marquette and Louis Joliet, the next Frenchmen to come through the area were the greatest of all French explorers, René-Robert Cavelier, Sieur de LaSalle; his faithful companion Henri de Tonti; and a contingent of 20–30 fellow Frenchmen and their families from Canada. Iroquois traders at Montreal had told LaSalle of a beautiful river to the south. LaSalle thought the river must flow into the "Gulf of California" and that he could reach China. He first explored the Ohio River and then portaged from Chicago through icy swamps. The men put their canoes on sleds, pushing and pulling their cargo many long miles on the icy Illinois River. The Illiniwek welcomed the French explorers, who helped them guard their territory against invading Iroquois war parties. The French were equally impressed by the Illiniwek and called them "the Illinois of the Rock."

Looking Down Illinois River from Summit of Starved Rock, State Park, Ottawa, Ill.

STARVED ROCK FROM THE ILLINOIS RIVER AND LOVER'S LEAP, *c.* **1930–1945.** LaSalle authorized construction of Fort St. Louis du Rocher, named for King Louis XIV, atop Starved Rock. Tonti oversaw the construction of the fort, which was built from 1682 to 1683. The fort was protected by a palisade and had several log and stone buildings, including a chapel and a magazine to hold arms and powder. The fort's design was made to fit the topography of the surface of the rock, and areas were used where the soil was securely anchored. When LaSalle, the fort's commander, was away from the fort, its trading post and the Illinois valley fur trade was run by his second in command, Henri de Tonti. For more than 20 years, Tonti lived at and fortified the fort. He resisted the English advances and continued running the trading post until 1702.

STARVED ROCK IN THE MOONLIGHT AND FROM THE ILLINOIS RIVER, C. 1900–1930.
René-Robert Cavelier, Sieur de LaSalle, called Starved Rock "the lone cliff." LaSalle had orders to build a chain of forts. The French, with Louis XIV as king, could then maintain their claim of the New World, which included the Illinois River valley and the Mississippi River valley. These forts would also aid them in keeping the English from expanding westward. Building Fort St. Louis on top of Starved Rock provided a commanding strategic position above the Illinois River. The fort became a center of French power and influence and a key French outpost. It also formed a nucleus for the first white settlement in the great west, the Mississippi valley, or Illinois.

A VIEW OF STARVED ROCK FROM THE NORTH SIDE OF THE ILLINOIS RIVER. The legend of Starved Rock is believed to have been a result of a war to avenge the death of Chief Pontiac of the Ottawa tribe. Pontiac was slain in 1769 by an Illiniwek while attending a tribal council in southern Illinois. A band of Illiniwek, pursued by their enemies, the Ottawa, the Potawatomi, the Kickapoo, and the Miami, took refuge on the one-half-acre summit of the rock. Surrounded, the Illiniwek were without food and water. As they lowered their buckets to the river below for water, their ropes were cut. After three weeks, the Illiniwek starved to death. Eleven of them escaped, took their enemies' canoes, and traveled to St. Louis. From then on the rock was known as Starved Rock.

THE AMERICAN FLAG ATOP STARVED ROCK, 1960. In 1835, Daniel F. Hitt purchased Starved Rock for $85. In 1891, he sold 265 acres at Starved Rock to Ferdinand Walther of Chicago for $21,000. Two local residents were instrumental in a campaign to develop Starved Rock into a state park. These two men were William Osman Jr., editor of the *Ottawa Free Trader*, and Horace Hull, an attorney and the LaSalle County circuit clerk. In December 1911, Ferdinand and Antoni Walther sold their holdings in Starved Rock to the State of Illinois for $146,000. This included property in the town of Science, among other properties. The state had appropriated $150,000 to be used for the park. This purchase was under the Scanlan–Johnson bill. Rep. W. M. Scanlan and Sen. Henry W. Johnson played an important role in the establishment of the park. Johnson lived at 630 East Main Street in Ottawa and was elected to the Illinois Senate in 1910. Starved Rock State Park opened under the supervision of the State Park Commission, headquartered at the park on May 1, 1911.

Two

A RIVER FLOWS BY

THE ILLINOIS RIVER AT STARVED ROCK, 1906. Steamboats first traveled on the Illinois River in 1828. "Traveling palaces" became popular in the 1840s. By the 1850s, over 59 steamboats were traveling on the Illinois River, transporting both passengers and farm produce. The steamboat's coal-powered engine turned the wooden paddlewheel as it propelled through the water. Coal was readily available in nearby towns along the river. There was considerable steamboat traffic between Peru and St. Louis even before the Illinois and Michigan Canal was completed in 1848. In the 1870s, the Illinois River was a sluggish stream with one rapid at Starved Rock and another at Marseilles. The river was deep enough for good size boats except at these rapids.

Illinois River Valley from top of Pulpit Rock, Lovers Leap in distance.
Midway between Starved Rock and Horse Shoe Canyon, near Ottawa, La Salle and Peru, Ills.

THE ILLINOIS RIVER FROM THE TOP OF PULPIT ROCK AND LOVER'S LEAP, C. 1907–1915.
An article in the *Henry Republican* illustrates the appeal of the river and the rock. On August 12, 1875, 300 passengers from Henry and Lacon left the dock at 7:00 a.m. for a cruise to Starved Rock on the *Grey Eagle*. Five bridges were passed on the route, at Henry, Peru, the wagon bridge at Shippingsport, the Illinois Central Railroad bridge, and a pontoon bridge at LaSalle. Passengers enjoyed the scenery along the Illinois River, catching up with old friends, and dancing en route. The *Grey Eagle* reached Starved Rock at noon. Hon. P. S. Perley, Rev. William Tracy, and Allen N. Ford gave impromptu speeches explaining the history of the rock. After a picnic lunch, everyone agreed on what an enjoyable and pleasant day was had by all.

7053. Illinois River from Lovers' Leap, LaSalle Co., Ill.

Illinois River East from top of Lovers Leap, State Park View, Starved Rock, Ill.

THE ILLINOIS RIVER EAST FROM LOVER'S LEAP AND WEST FROM STARVED ROCK, C. 1915–1930.
Settlers made claims, built cabins, and were living on each side of the river in 1830. John Hayes lived in Peru, Samuel Lapsley and Burton Ayers in LaSalle, and George Brown, Dr. David Walker, and Elmer Weed in Ottawa. The town of Science was on both sides of the river at Starved Rock and Utica. A bridge over the Illinois River linked the two sides of Science in the early 1800s. It was laid out and surveyed in 1838 by Daniel F. Hitt, the surveyor for LaSalle County. The trustees for the county then were Simon Crosiar, W. Clayton, and John Wallace. Science still appeared on a 1929 map of LaSalle County. As Utica grew, Science became a ghost town.

LOOKING DOWN THE ILLINOIS RIVER FROM THE MOUTH OF HORSESHOE CANYON, c. 1907–1915. The streams from the canyons empty into the Illinois River at their mouths. The bottom of the Illinois River is composed of sand and clay silt, sometimes as much as 50 feet thick. The outflow of water from canyon runoff contributes to this.

View from Top of Starved Rock, looking West, State Park View, Starved Rock, Ill.

THE ILLINOIS RIVER LOOKING WEST FROM THE TOP OF STARVED ROCK, c. 1915–1930. The Illinois River is formed at the junction of the DesPlaines and the Kankakee Rivers. It flows 273 miles southwest to the Mississippi River. The river played an important part in the Native Americans' and French traders' lives, as it was the principal water route connecting the Great Lakes with the Mississippi River.

LOOKING EAST FROM LOVER'S LEAP, C. 1915–1930. There are many attractions in Starved Rock State Park, including woods, canyons, historic battlegrounds, and miles of trails, but these may all pale in comparison to some of the many beautiful river views. The gentleman pictured on the postcard found a perfect spot to enjoy the river views and study his map of the park to plan his next adventure.

The Illinois Valley from Top of "Starved Rock" near La Salle, Ill.

THE VIEW FROM THE TOP OF STARVED ROCK, 1921. Fr. Jacques Marquette wrote, "There are no grounds on earth superior in fertility and productiveness than those that can be found for miles on each side of the Illinois River." The Native Americans grew corn or maize and garden produce in the fertile soil of Plum Island in the Illinois River near Starved Rock. Archaeologists believe a massacre took place on Plum Island long ago.

MOONLIGHT ON THE ILLINOIS RIVER, C. 1930–1945. The water sparkles in the silvery reflection of the moon from the quiet waters of the Illinois River. The *Spirit of Peoria* steamboat today makes the 150-mile round-trip between Starved Rock and Peoria. A romantic dinner on the deck of the boat while traveling on the Illinois River in the moonlight is a pleasurable experience.

ILLINOIS RIVER FROM SUMMIT OF STARVED ROCK, STARVED ROCK STATE PARK, ILL.—16

THE ILLINOIS RIVER FROM THE SUMMIT OF STARVED ROCK, C. 1930–1945. In his journal, Henri de Tonti recorded that spectacular catfish were caught in the Illinois River near Fort St. Louis. One specimen was large enough to feed 22 of his men. The Illinois River today is one of the best sports fishing rivers in the country. Various types of fish caught are sauger, walleye, crappies, carp, bullhead, catfish, large and smallmouth bass, white bass, and stripers.

A View of the Illinois River, 1970. The Illinois River is 17,000 years old. Most of the Illinois valley that it flows through is nearly 900,000 years old. The valley is really two valleys in one, the 65.5-mile-long upper valley of recent origin and the 207-mile-long lower valley inherited from a previous stream. These two valleys meet in the vicinity of Hennepin.

View from the Shore of the Illinois River, 1960. Trees shade the banks, and sandstone bluffs line either side of the Illinois River. Much of the rest of the area is a flat, gently rolling plain. The upland prairies were created during an intense warming period several thousand years after the glaciers melted. The Illinois River valley near Starved Rock is a sharp contrast to the nearby flatland.

Iroquois passing Eagles Cliff, Starved Rock State Park, Illinois

THE IROQUOIS EXCURSION BOAT ON THE ILLINOIS RIVER, 1940S. For years, tourists have enjoyed Starved Rock State Park whether on boat or bike. On August 15, 1901, the Lincoln Cycling Club, with Edward A. Price Jr. as captain, visited the famed resort with 35 of its 300 members. This club was one of the finest cycling clubs in the country. The members came down by train from Chicago to Starved Rock, bringing their wheels. The captain, accompanied by C. A. Curry, Carl F. Mayer, Albert E. Schad, and Fred C. Schad, left the train at Ottawa and proceeded by wheel through Utica to Starved Rock. The rest of the members continued on the train to Utica. According to the *Ottawa Republican Times,* "The gentlemen seemed to enjoy all the beauties and benefits that can be extracted from the pure air, and wholesome environments of the country. The club's purpose is sociability and the improvement of the heart and intellect by broadening their acquaintances with mankind and nature."

Three

MANY PATHS TO TAKE

ALONG THE ROAD FROM STARVED ROCK TO DEER PARK, 1914. Deer Park is a short distance south of Starved Rock. Large herds of deer were often captured by the local Native Americans in this area, giving it the name Deer Park. The deer were attracted to this area because of the many mineral springs that they used as salt licks. Today it is known as Matthiessen State Park. Frederick Matthiessen, a local industrialist and philanthropist, purchased 176 acres in the 1890s. Upon his death, the park was donated to the State of Illinois. Matthiessen employed many men to build bridges, stairways, and trails in developing his private park. Roads were constructed between the two popular parks so visitors could easily travel to both, as shown in this postcard.

Main Entrance to
Starved Rock State Park, Illinois.—8

THE MAIN PARK ENTRANCE TO STARVED ROCK STATE PARK, C. 1915–1930. Starved Rock has been a popular destination for many years. According to the *Ottawa Republican Times* in June 1901, the Galesburg Retail Merchants Association visited Starved Rock. The group had dinner at the Starved Rock Hotel, climbed to the top of Starved Rock, saw Lover's Leap, and explored French Canyon.

MAIN ENTRANCE TO STARVED ROCK STATE PARK, ILL.—18

ANOTHER VIEW OF THE MAIN ENTRANCE TO THE PARK, C. 1930–1945. Some of the prairie plants that can been seen along the roadways in the park are New England aster, black-eyed Susan, coreopsis, purple coneflower, and goldenrod. The yellow and brown black-eyed Susan is probably the most common and well-recognized wildflower. Birds love to eat the seed heads of the purple coneflower in the winter.

THE WEST ENTRANCE TO STARVED ROCK STATE PARK, C. 1907–1915. The park has three road entrances. The west entrance is near the bridge over the Illinois River, or a mile south of Utica. The east entrance starts near the Salt Well Point, six miles west of Ottawa. The south entrance is one mile directly south of the rock.

WEST ENTRANCE DRIVE TO STARVED ROCK STATE PARK, C. 1915–1930. In *Wild and Scenic Illinois,* Willard Clay and Debra Alsvig-Clay said, "This area—consisting of Starved Rock and Matthiessen State Parks, together with a significant portion of the Illinois River corridor and a million or so acres of surrounding native prairie—ranks as one of our favorites in the nation to visit and photograph."

ANOTHER VIEW OF THE WEST ENTRANCE, *c.* **1907–1915.** Upon entering Starved Rock State Park at the west entrance, the high massive rock walls on one side and the dense woods on the other entice the visitor to continue following the road. Excitement builds as a curve is approached in anticipation of the beautiful scenery that lies ahead.

FOLLOW THE ROAD TO STARVED ROCK STATE PARK, *c.* **1930–1945.** The partially shady road from Ottawa to Starved Rock is a beautiful drive extending part of the way along the Illinois River. The very deep canyons of Horseshoe, Tonti, and LaSalle can be seen from Route 71, and visitors will notice some lovely St. Peter sandstone formations.

THE PATHWAY LEADING TO LOVER'S LEAP AT STARVED ROCK, 1909. During the Edwardian era, skirts and white blouses were very popular and are worn by two of the four women in this postcard. Because women wished to mimic the Gibson girl look, they would embroider their high-neck blouses or add lace trim and a brooch.

HENNEPIN CANYON FROM CANYON DRIVE, C. 1907–1915. Hennepin Canyon is named for Fr. Louis Hennepin, a "Black Robe." The Native Americans called the Jesuit priests "Black Robes" because they wore long black robes. The Jesuits' mission was to teach Christianity and to spread the Catholic religion to the Native Americans.

THE STAIRWAY LEADING TO LOVER'S LEAP AT STARVED ROCK, C. 1915–1930. The *Ottawa Republican Times* reported that in July 1901 a group from the University of Chicago toured the area. An excursion train with four full coaches was run from Chicago to Utica. Lover's Leap was just one of the sites the group visited in the park that day.

ALONG THE OLD NATIVE AMERICAN TRAIL AT STARVED ROCK STATE PARK, C. 1915–1930. The old Native American trail leads to high bluffs, cliffs, gulches, canyons, valleys, the riverbank, and elsewhere in the park. Today at the park, colored posts that correlate with maps on brochures are placed along the trails, helping to guide the hiker along the trails.

ANOTHER VIEW OF THE STAIRWAY LEADING TO LOVER'S LEAP, C. 1930–1945. Erosion is one of the biggest problems the park faces. Visitors can help prevent erosion by staying on the paths. The planks and staircases around Starved Rock State Park were built to prevent the effects of erosion. Natural erosion caused by water and wind cannot be protected against.

ENTRANCE TO WILDCAT CANYON IN STARVED ROCK STATE PARK, C. 1907–1915. This postcard shows some of the many beautiful plants and wildflowers that bloom in the canyons and forested areas, such as lichens, mosses, wild iris, trillium, marsh marigolds, Dutchman's breeches, spiderworts, shooting star, columbine, phlox, violets, spring beauties, May apples, skunk cabbage with its distinctive aroma, and many more.

ONE OF THE MANY TRAILS IN HORSESHOE CANYON, C. 1930–1945. Some of the more readily accessible canyons have well-defined paths, stairs at the points of more difficult ascent, and bridges to cross brooks that make their way along the canyon beds.

A PATH FROM THE HOTEL LEADING TO WILDCAT AND HORSESHOE CANYONS, C. 1907–1915. The fresh green colors of the spring and the vibrant red and yellow colors of the fall show a stark contrast to the white blanket of snow in the winter. This ever-changing environment makes the park an ideal place to visit no matter what time of year.

Bridge at Horseshoe Canyon, Starved Rock State Park, Illinois

AN ARCHED FOOTBRIDGE AT HORSESHOE CANYON IN STARVED ROCK, 1939–1960. This is a view from an excursion boat on the Illinois River. This view shows the charming, rustic wooden arched bridge built by the Civilian Conservation Corps (CCC) in 1936. The slight slope of the bridge helps its strength and increases the safety of visitors not wishing to slip on its slope.

ANOTHER VIEW OF THE BRIDGE AT HORSESHOE CANYON CREEK, 1963. This arched footbridge spans the canyon and provides a spot to rest and take in the surroundings. At times, while pausing on the bridge, raccoons and squirrels can be seen searching for nuts and berries. White-tailed deer, wild cottontail rabbits, and mosquitoes may also be noticed. Beavers and muskrats can sometimes be seen along the river trails.

A Model T on the Rustic Bridge at Horseshoe Canyon, 1914. Henry Ford built the first Model T in 1908. He paid assembly line workers an unheard of $5 a day for eight hours of work. By 1921, Ford had produced more than five million tin lizzies, or flivvers as they were sometimes called. The Model T manufactured from 1908 to 1927 "put America on wheels" because of its affordable cost of $850.

Men Posing on a Bridge at Starved Rock, 1908. The men posing on the bridge are wearing the typical styles of the time, which were long slim trousers and lightweight cotton shirts. The men of the CCC partially built the lodge, stairways, shelters, and bridges and developed new trails in the park. This rustic bridge was built long before the days of the corps.

A Rustic Bridge Leading to the Canyons, *c. 1907–1915.* Starved Rock State Park was placed on the National Register of Historic Places in 1966. The years 1650 to 1699 are those listed as its major period of significance. These were the years of the early missionaries and explorers and, of course, the many Native Americans who flourished in the area.

A Rustic Bridge near French Canyon, *c. 1907–1915.* This rustic footbridge allowed trail passage over canyon waterways. Just a few miles east of this footbridge, the first bridge built on the Illinois River was built at LaSalle Street in Ottawa. This Ottawa bridge was built around 1855 for about $60,000.

THE STAIRCASE LEADING TO THE TOP OF STARVED ROCK, C. 1915–1930. On these steep steps and the only trail to the top of the rock, a Native American named "Indian Sam" sold beaded jewelry that he had made. He lived at the park all year long, and on Sundays during the summer, he wore his Native American clothing for visitors. In the 1920s, the trail was improved to make it more accessible and the stairs easier to ascend. Once reached, the top of the rock is covered with trees and bushes and offers a lovely view of the curvy shores of the Illinois River. It is easy to understand why Starved Rock made an ideal site for Fort St. Louis. Three sides of the rock are nearly vertical and difficult to climb. The fourth side had a narrow path up a steep wall and would have been the only avenue of approach for an enemy. This allowed for concentration of firepower, making the rock easily defendable.

Four

HARNESSING THE RIVER

THE STARVED ROCK LOCK AND DAM, C. 1930–1945. The Starved Rock Lock and Dam is located at the Illinois Waterway Visitor Center near Utica and directly across the Illinois River from Starved Rock. The Illinois Waterway Visitor Center, which opened on July 16, 1978, has many exhibits on the waterway and an observation deck that overlooks the lock and dam. The observation deck is the best place to watch boats and barges passing through the locks. A slide show explaining the history of the waterway and how the locking process works is shown in the auditorium.

THE DAM AT STARVED ROCK, C. 1930–1945. Before the dam was built, the Illinois River varied from 350 to 1,000 feet wide and had a gentle current. Travel on the Illinois River was difficult as well since the water averaged 18 inches in depth. The Illinois and Michigan Canal terminating at Peru bypassed the shallow areas, allowing transportation by water from Lake Michigan to the Mississippi River. After the dam was built, the river width varied from 350 feet wide at Peoria Street in Peru to 3,875 feet wide at Starved Rock Marina east of the dam. Knowing that the Illinois and Michigan canal was obsolete in 1908, the people of Illinois approved a $20 million bond issue. Leading the movement in Ottawa for digging a channel and building locks for a new waterway were Richard Jordan, hardware merchant, Judge H. M. Johnson, and Mayor Al Schock.

LOVERS LEAP, ILLINOIS RIVER AND DAM, STARVED ROCK STATE PARK, ILL.—21

THE STARVED ROCK DAM IN DAYLIGHT AND MOONLIGHT, C. 1930–1945. The Illinois Waterway Project was enacted by Congress to provide a permanent nine-foot-deep navigable channel between the Great Lakes and the Mississippi River for commercial boat traffic. The Great Lakes to the Gulf Waterway Project with its locks and dams began on November 20, 1920, and was completed on May 31, 1933, at a cost of $4.4 million. Operated by the U.S. Army Corps of Engineers, the Illinois Waterway division of the project opened on March 4, 1933. On opening day, the boat *Kno Mac Se* chartered by the *Ottawa Republican Times* made the 12-hour trip to Chicago. It carried art glass from Peltier Glass Factory, cucumbers from the Kay-Bee Company, and various products from Ottawa Silica Company, Midwest Brick Company, and other Ottawa establishments.

LOVER'S LEAP AND THE STARVED ROCK DAM, 1940. During World War II, over 1,200 war vessels built on the Great Lakes passed through the locks. There were 28 large submarines and 72 cargo vessels, each with a 5,000-ton capacity. East of the lock and dam along the river near Seneca over 150 landing ship tanks were built during this war. These vessels contributed greatly to the war effort.

VIEW OF THE LOCK AND DAM FROM LOVER'S LEAP, 1958. The Starved Rock Lock and Dam Historic District was placed on the National Register of Historic Places in 2004. The years listed as its major period of significance are 1925 to 1949. The register is part of a national program to "coordinate and support public and private efforts to identify, evaluate and protect our historic and archeological resources."

EAGLES CLIFF WITH THE STARVED ROCK DAM IN THE BACKGROUND, 1940S. The waterway is open 24 hours per day 365 days per year. The Northwest Ordinance (1787) allows boats to lock through the river at no charge. Priority is given as to which vessels shall pass first through the locks. Warships have top priority, followed by mail ships, commercial passenger boats, barges, and pleasure boats, in that order.

War Chief passing Dam in Upper Pool, Starved Rock State Park, Illinois

THE *WAR CHIEF* AT THE STARVED ROCK DAM, 1940S. Various excursion boats operated on the Illinois River giving tours for visitors. One item of interest pointed out to visitors was that during dredging operations on the Illinois Waterway, an old brass cannon, thought to be one from Fort St. Louis, was recovered from the riverbed.

STARVED ROCK WITH THE DAM IN THE BACKGROUND, 1955. The locks can handle eight barges and a tow with cargo weighing over 12,000 tons at a time. A barge can carry 1,500 tons, and one tugboat can push 15 barges at a time. Each tugboat and its barges travel approximately seven miles per hour, and about 10 tugs and their barges per day pass through the locks at Starved Rock.

EAGLES CLIFF WITH THE LOCK AND DAM IN THE DISTANCE, 1930s. On the Illinois River lock and dams are found at Marseilles, Starved Rock, Peoria, near Beardstown, and at Grafton. Additional sets are found at Joliet on the Des Plains River, at Lockport on the Chicago Ship and Sanitary Canal, and at Alton on the Mississippi River. These form the connection between the Great Lakes and the Mississippi River, and ultimately the Gulf of Mexico.

A View of the Dam from Lover's Leap, 1940s. The dam is 1,272 feet long, and all seven locks are 110 feet wide and 600 feet long. A vessel en route from Lake Michigan to the Mississippi River is lowered on a series of steps varying from 40 feet at Lockport to 19 feet at Starved Rock. The locking process works like this: As a tugboat and a barge enter the empty lock from the downriver side, the lock doors close. The lock is flooded and the tug and barge are raised up to the river height. The second lock door is opened and the tug pushes the barge out of the lock and continues on the river. The process of locking through takes about 20 minutes for a boat but can take up to two hours or longer depending upon the number of barges. Each year over 45 million tons of coal, gravel, sand, corn, soybeans, fertilizer, cement, iron products, chemicals, petroleum products, grain, and sulfur pass through the locks.

STARVED ROCK WITH THE DAM IN THE BACKGROUND, 1960S. Starved Rock Lock and Dam was built on a sandstone ledge in the Illinois River. In July 1730, 350 Fox warriors and their families forded the Illinois River west of Starved Rock at this ledge and joined the Iroquois to the southeast in Deer Park Township. The Fox were attacked by the French, who wanted to take control of the Illinois valley. This ledge was also used as a fording spot for stagecoaches carrying passengers to Springfield. Abraham Lincoln probably forded the river at this point as he traveled the Illinois circuit. Lincoln may have also passed through the park in 1832 as he moved from one Black Hawk war fort to another to be sworn in or out of service. He served in three different outfits for three months. On August 21, 1858, Abraham Lincoln, also known as "Honest Abe," and Stephen Douglas, known as "the Little Giant," were in the area to take part in the first of their seven debates in Washington Square in Ottawa.

Five

THE STARVED
ROCK HOTEL

THE STARVED ROCK HOTEL ENTRANCE, 1908. A hotel stood upon the high ground within a few hundred feet of the Illinois River and just west of the base of Starved Rock. The front of the hotel offered a beautiful view of the Illinois River and was a convenient location for guests arriving by boat. The hotel was built in the Victorian style similar to an American clapboard seaside cottage, which was perfect for its location. The Queen Anne style of the hotel that was popular at the time is easily identified by steeply pitched slate roofs, an irregular shape, front facing gables, fish scale shingles in the eaves, double hung windows with the upper panel having several smaller panes, large porches or verandas, and tall chimneys.

THE ENTRANCE AND THE HOTEL, 1907. By January 1890, the Starved Rock Hotel was ready for shingling. An artesian well was 250 feet deep and already yielded a fair flow of water with plans to dig the well deeper. Matthew Bungart had the contract for the plumbing and gas fitting, and Edward Grube had the contract for the painting and decorating. Plans were made for a platform or observatory, 24 feet high, to be erected on top of the rock. It was to be enclosed by a railing on which a flagstaff bearing the stars and stripes could be seen for miles around. The hotel was three stories high, and a broad veranda extended on three sides. It was 105 feet across the front and 100 feet deep. Four three-room cottages were located near the rear of the hotel.

THE STARVED ROCK HOTEL AND GROUNDS, C. 1907–1915. The hotel was lit with gas and had 100 guest rooms. Each large and well-furnished room had electricity and running water. All rooms included three meals per day, and the dining hall seated 250 guests. Tennis courts built for $2,500 were near the hotel. Also separate from the hotel was a clubhouse designed for dancing, music, bowling, and other amusements. It was far enough away as to not disturb those who preferred the quiet rest and relaxation of the resort. In 1900, the first-class hotel with all its modern conveniences advertised first-class hotel rooms for $3 per day and second-class rooms for $2 per day or $10 to $15 per week. One knew their roommate in first class, but in second class one shared a room with whoever else needed a room.

STARVED ROCK HOTEL AND SURROUNDINGS NEAR OTTAWA, UTICA AND LA SALLE, ILL.

THE STARVED ROCK HOTEL, 1907. Across the river from the Starved Rock Hotel was a hotel built in 1832 and at various times was called the Half-Way House or the Sulphur Springs Hotel. It had 30-inch-thick stone walls, 28 guest rooms, and a ballroom and a theater on the third floor. A sulfur spring with water thought to be good for one's health was located on the grounds. Jenny Lind, the "Swedish Nightingale" who was brought to America by P. T. Barnum, was said to have sung there. Abraham Lincoln is believed to have stayed at Half-Way House, a tavern and a stopping station halfway between Chicago and Peoria on the Frink and Walker Stage Coach Line. This stagecoach line was one of the busiest in Illinois. As many as eight four-horse carriages per day were run between Chicago and Peru. Passengers would board steamboats at Peru for the trip down the Illinois River to the Mississippi River. The depth of the Illinois River only allowed boats to go as far as Peru. Half-Way House sat on a 267-acre farm. After the lock and dam was built, 100 acres were flooded by the dam's backwater pool, forever burying part of the site of the Kaskaskia village.

THE STARVED ROCK HOTEL AND CLUBHOUSE, 1915. According to the *Ottawa Free Trader*, an account of a life in a simpler time was printed on July 3, 1891. The Clover Club gave a party at Starved Rock. Members and their lady friends arrived from Ottawa shortly after 7:00 p.m. Edward Grube, the hotel's landlord, informed them that the hotel was their property for the night. The dining room was cleared of furniture and converted into a dancing hall. The guests danced until midnight when supper was served. At 2:30 a.m. the evening ended. Some of the guests in attendance were John Dougherty, T. F. Quinn, Nellie Kelly, Robert Carr, George Holmes, James Dougherty, Robert Richardson, Will P. Leahy, Tim Looney, James Gentleman, Frank Ayers, Mary Hadley, Annie Quinn, Katie Riordan, Carrie Formhals, Nellie White, Nannie Cassidy, Alice McLane, Mollie Morrissey, Kittie Casey, J. E. Skelly, John Duncan, James Shelton, John McNulty, Oliver Holmes, Frank Leahy, Will McKay, Annie and Tillie Garrity, Kit Walsh, Maggie McGuire, Emma and Theresa Bungart, Tessie Scott, Maggie Stewart, Fannie Moeller, and Frieda Fiber.

THE STARVED ROCK HOTEL AND SURROUNDINGS, C. 1915–1930. Edward Grube, a local painting contractor, was the first manager of the hotel in 1891. In 1897, William Tatsch from Hoffman House in New York City managed it. C. H. Geyer of Chicago was the manager in 1901. The *Ottawa Republican Times* printed, "He came well recommended and seems to be the right man according to reports which come from that region."

THE HOTEL AND SURROUNDINGS, 1932. A typical season at the Starved Rock Hotel ran from May 15 until October 1. Cars of the Chicago, Ottawa and Peoria system carried signs advertising Starved Rock as a destination. Passengers could reach Starved Rock by taking the Chicago, Ottawa and Peoria Railroad. The interurban went as far as Joliet. Chicago passengers then transferred to the Chicago, Joliet, and Elgin line.

54

The Entrance to the Starved Rock Hotel, *c.* **1907–1915.** This postcard was published by Kneussl Brothers, which ran a drugstore in Ottawa. Its motto was, "not how cheap but how good." Besides drugs, the store carried books, stationery, and wallpaper and did picture framing. The Kneussl Brothers printed thousands of postcards at the beginning of the 20th century showing scenes of Ottawa, Starved Rock, and many other scenes in LaSalle County.

Starved Rock Hotel, 1932. In 1910, the Essanay Movie Studio of Chicago filmed mostly western movies at Starved Rock. Some of the bluffs around Starved Rock as well as some of the streets in Utica were used as a backdrop for the films. The cast, which included Gloria Swanson, stayed at the Starved Rock Hotel. The glamorous "queen of the silent movies" reached stardom just a few years later.

THE HOTEL VERANDA, 1914. At the beginning of the 20th century, all adults wore hats in public. Men tipped their hats when meeting a lady and removed them inside. Around 1910, a trim, simpler hat replaced large-brimmed, plume-festooned hats held with a long pin for ladies. Straw hats, a summertime favorite, were lighter and a good choice for attending a summer band concert on the Starved Rock Hotel veranda.

THE RIVERFRONT AT STARVED ROCK, C. 1907–1915. This image could have been captured from Plum Island, which is located in the Illinois River across from the rock. During the 1960s, airplane rides were available from this island for visitors. A cable car near Starved Rock transported visitors to the island. Planes then took off from the island for a bird's-eye view of the park and the Illinois Valley.

Capt. Seth Ballard's Passenger Steamer *Lola* on the Illinois River, 1907. After retiring as a boat captain, Ballard built a hotel on Motor Inn Island near Starved Rock. Visitors rang a bell at the landing, and a boat was sent from the hotel to take guests to the island. A gambling saloon was located on the first floor. This island was flooded when the Starved Rock Lock and Dam was completed.

The Starved Rock Ferry Company and Landing, c. 1907–1915. Train passengers from Chicago to Utica paid $4.90 round-trip on the Chicago, Rock Island, and Pacific Railroad. Thomas Manley, owner of Manley's Livery in Utica, shuttled visitors by horse and carriage to the Starved Rock ferry and then back to the railroad station. His business became Manley's Garage when the horseless carriage became the norm.

THE BOAT LANDING FROM THE STARVED ROCK HOTEL, C. 1907–1915. On July 18, 1901, a Mr. Langford, who controlled a line of steamers between Peru and Peoria, was in Ottawa. He needed to ascertain that the Illinois River channel was deep enough to safely propel a steamer between Ottawa and Starved Rock. He felt such a line would not only be profitable, but visitors would enjoy the beautiful scenery between Ottawa and Starved Rock.

THE RIVER ENTRANCE TO THE STARVED ROCK HOTEL, C. 1915–1930. Thousands attended outdoor performances of the drama *Tonti* at the foot of Starved Rock in August 1896. There were large excursions from Chicago, Joliet, Ottawa, Rock Island, Geneso, LaSalle, and Peru. The costumes were 16th-century French, and those of the Native Americans were mainly of paint and feathers. The play was written by Henry Merker of the *Illinois Staats-Zeitung*, a Chicago German American newspaper.

RIVERFRONT AT STARVED ROCK, C. 1907–1915. The Starved Rock ferries were busy on September 5, 1901, as one of the largest excursions ever came to Utica from Blue Island and Joliet. Sixteen coaches and a baggage car were crowded with 1,113 passengers. Buses, hacks, carriages, drays, and hayracks were used to transport the crowd to the ferries for their trip across the Illinois River to Starved Rock.

THE CAMPGROUND AT STARVED ROCK, LASALLE COUNTY, ILL.

THE CAMPGROUND AT STARVED ROCK, 1911. In the 1900s, roads, trails, and parking lots were laid out, concessions stands and restrooms were built, and a campground on the bluff east of the hotel was established. In the 1930s, a new campground on the lower level of the park near the Illinois River was set up as it was larger and more convenient for guests. Camping became very popular as cars and roads improved.

STARVED ROCK LANDING, 1912. In the 1920s, Starved Rock could be reached by the Rock Island System. Six trains a day traveled to Utica, and five trains per day went from Utica to Chicago. An autobus took the passengers to the rock from the station. L. W. Hess, of Ottawa, who was in charge of the ferry landing, encouraged visitors to take the ferryboats to the park and the hotel.

Returning to Starved Rock, Starved Rock State Park, Illinois

A TOUR BOAT COMPLETES THE TOUR OF STARVED ROCK, 1930s. Numerous excursion boats were operated from nearby docks to take visitors up the river to see features not visible or accessible from land. The Starved Rock Scenic Boat Company sold round-trip tickets printed by the Arcus Ticket Company. One of the favorite stops was to the remote Horseshoe Canyon. The boat trip saved the hiker from walking miles of trails through rough terrain.

Ferry Landing at Starved Rock, State Park,
near Ottawa, Utica and La Salle, Ill.

THE FERRY LANDING AT STARVED ROCK, 1915. In the 1890s, health spas and resort hotels gained popularity. Visitors found Starved Rock to be an ideal summer resort, without having to travel far for rest and recreation. Their daily routine may have included a round of sightseeing, wandering amid the secluded canyons, or resting in the cool shade of the stately pines. Fishing and boating on the river were also favorite pastimes.

SOUVENIR AND POST CARD STAND AT STARVED ROCK, LASALLE COUNTY, ILL.

THE SOUVENIR AND POSTCARD STAND AT STARVED ROCK, 1911. In 1914, Nicholas Spiros, of LaSalle, was in charge of the souvenir concessions for the park. William Jasper, another popular concessionaire, was promoted and placed in charge of the dance hall in the 1920s. Around this time, postcards were printed with a divided back, allowing the sender to write both the address and a message without defacing the scenic picture on the front.

VIEW OF THE DANCE HALL FROM THE SOUTH CLIFF, C. 1915–1930. Guests danced away the evenings doing the tango, the rumba, the samba, the fox-trot, and the swing. Some of the bands that played at the dance pavilion on Saturday nights and midweek were led by Wayne King, Rudy Valle, Guy Lombardo, Benny Goodman, and Duke Ellington. Admission was a nickel for men and no charge for women.

THE BATHING POOL AT STARVED ROCK, 1928. Near the Starved Rock Hotel was a bathing pool. The pool was fed by a 955-foot-deep artesian well that provided a constant flow of freshwater. A wall of concrete circled the pool, and an island or beach in the center of the pool was used for sunbathing. This beach was also used at night for night bathing under a floodlight.

THE BATHING POOL AND BATHHOUSE AT STARVED ROCK, 1914. Henry Norton supervised the bathing beach in 1914. A bathhouse nearby provided a convenient changing area for the guests. About the time of this postcard, ladies' bathing suits were considered shocking and all-revealing. The suits were a sleeveless, figure-hugging wool tank suit. The suit was actually very similar to the male suit. A bathing cap was usually worn by women.

VISITORS GATHERING TO WATCH THE SWIMMERS, 1914. Women's hemlines rose dramatically to mid-calf about the time of this postcard. Women became more active getting in and out of cars, and material was saved for World War I. In 1918, a miniature locomotive was purchased from Lincoln Park in Chicago to circle the pool. In the 1940s, the swimming pool was filled in as it had many leaks.

THE CHILDREN'S PLAYGROUND AT STARVED ROCK, 1914. At the time of this postcard, playgrounds were a relatively new idea that was quickly viewed as necessary for children's health and well-being. The playground for children at Starved Rock State Park was equipped with a merry-go-round, teeter-totters, swings, slides, and sand piles. A large lawn provided an area for playing ball, tag, croquet, and other lawn games. Nearby shade trees provided a cool place to rest.

THE PICNIC GROUNDS AT STARVED ROCK, 1914. Paper cups and napkins were fairly new supplies for picnickers in 1914. Sandwiches were "the backbone of all out-of-door luncheons." Many church and Sunday school groups held picnics at Starved Rock. August 8, 1901, was one such picnic day at Starved Rock. An article in the *Ottawa Republican Times* said, "It must have also been pastor's day by the number of clergymen present!"

THE BOATHOUSE AT STARVED ROCK, C. 1915–1930. The boathouse was a permanent wooden structure along the Illinois River where boats were boarded, docked, and stored. Handmade wooden rowboats were made available to let for $3 per day. Rowing was a popular, healthy, physically demanding outdoor activity.

THE RESTAURANT AT STARVED ROCK STATE PARK, 1939. This postcard dates to the time when students at Harvard University were perfecting the fad of swallowing goldfish, Judy Garland was starring in *The Wizard of Oz*, and Al Capone was released from Alcatraz. Visitors came from far and near to relax and enjoy themselves at Starved Rock State Park on the Illinois River, and many enjoyed a fine meal in the restaurant.

THE SOUVENIR AND REFRESHMENT STAND AT STARVED ROCK, 1970s. W. E. Crosiar was awarded the contract for concessions at the park in April 1912. Crosiar was promoted to the general manager of the hotel and the park in 1918. An old advertisement for Starved Rock said, "Do not fail to visit, The Scenic Wonderland of the West at Starved Rock State Park. Good Roads, Bathing, Boating, Dancing. First Class hotel accommodations are under the management of W.E. Crosiar, Utica, Ill." Under his management, 40,000 people visited Starved Rock State Park on Labor Day 1923, and 5,000 people were turned away. By 1924, Crosiar had built a bathhouse, a bathing pool, and an artesian well.

Six

STARVED ROCK LODGE

THE ROAD TO STARVED ROCK LODGE, 1939. Starved Rock Lodge is one of the finest examples of modern park buildings in the Midwest. Its rustic and stone appearance helps it to blend into the park's landscape as it sets majestically on a bluff overlooking the Illinois River and Starved Rock. Starved Rock Lodge and cabins were added to the National Register of Historic Places in 1985. Joseph F. Booten is listed as the architect, builder, or engineer, and its major period of significance is from 1925 to 1949. The cost to build the lodge and cabins was $200,000 to $300,000. Later a 48-room addition was completed costing $200,000. In 1986–1988, a $4 million renovation and addition was completed. This renovation included a 30-room addition, an indoor heated swimming pool, and improvements to the original buildings.

THE EXTERIOR OF STARVED ROCK LODGE, 1940s. In 1933, Pres. Franklin Delano Roosevelt began a program to put men back to work called the Civilian Conservation Corps (CCC), which was part of the New Deal campaign. In a time of great unemployment, thousands of men worked, making about $30 per month. They kept $5 for themselves, and the rest was sent home to their families to help out. They worked five days per week and were given three meals per day, a place to live, clothing, medical attention, and some education. The men were housed in tents upon arrival at Starved Rock until wooden barracks were built. The camps were run by the U.S. Army. Three companies were assigned to Starved Rock State Park. One group set up camp at Parkman Plain near Starved Rock, and another had its barracks in the lower level of the park. These buildings were later taken over by the state to be used for the park custodian services.

THE ENTRANCE TO STARVED ROCK LODGE, 1939. By 1935, over 2,650 camps of the CCC were in every state in the nation. One major purpose of the program was tree planting. The group of men that planted trees was known as "Roosevelt's Tree Army." Three million men of the CCC renewed the nation's forests and helped erosion by planting three billion trees. In Illinois alone, over 60 million trees were planted. Millions of acres of federal and state properties were improved. In the 1930s, Starved Rock Lodge was built in part by the CCC. Records for the CCC show lists of nationwide work sites. One of the three camps for Starved Rock State Park is listed as SP-23, 1609, 12/15/1933, Utica. SP-23 is the number given by the state to the project and the camp, 1609 is the number given by the federal government to each company, and 12/15/33 is the date the company occupied that particular camp. Utica was the closest town that had a railroad stop and a post office.

ANOTHER EXTERIOR VIEW OF THE LODGE, 1940S. Joseph F. Booten, the architect for the Starved Rock Lodge, was chief of design and architecture for the State of Illinois. Other projects, including White Pines State Park Lodge and Cabins in Mount Morris, Old Graue Mill in Oak Brook, Black Hawk Museum and Lodge in Rock Island, and Pere Marquette State Park Lodge and Cabins in Grafton, were also completed by Booten.

TEPEE HOUSE AT STARVED ROCK, 1940S. Several cabins like the one pictured and limestone shelters were built by the CCC. The cabins and lodge were operated on the American plan. The American plan is a hotel term for a room that includes three meals per day, as opposed to the European plan where the rates cover only the room.

70

STARVED ROCK LODGE VERANDA AND VIEW, 1940s. A long porch or veranda along the rear of the lodge overlooks the visitor center, the Illinois River valley, Starved Rock, and the Illinois River. This area is a great place to sit and rest and to enjoy the outdoors and the panoramic view.

STARVED ROCK LODGE VERANDA. The $4.5 million visitor's center built in 2001 just down the staircase from the veranda includes many exhibits explaining the story of the historic rock. Some of the various exhibits in the visitor's center include a diorama of Fort St. Louis, a three-dimensional exhibit of Starved Rock State Park, an aquarium filled with Illinois River fish, and a movie theater.

THE GRAND HALL OF STARVED ROCK LODGE, 1970s. White pine brought from Indiana was used in the construction of the lodge. The full timbers shown in this postcard of the lodge mimic the rustic style used in the construction of the National Park Service lodges. This huge lounge, or great hall, of the lodge with its colorful furnishings is an inviting place for guests and friends to gather.

THE MAJESTIC FIREPLACE IN STARVED ROCK LODGE, 1960s. The massive rustic, double-sided fireplace in the lodge was built by the CCC. These men hauled 250 tons of Joliet limestone from Lemont to Starved Rock to build the fireplace. Additional stone was also used for the chimneys and the foundation. Millions of visitors each year pass though the great hall and admire its majestic fireplace.

ORIGINAL FURNISHINGS IN THE GREAT HALL, 1940s. The lodge interior has first-class accommodations, original furnishings, and peaceful surroundings. The furniture built by the men of the CCC was made from white oak. The bark of the white oak tree is light gray while that of the black oak is dark in color.

A COZY CORNER OF THE GREAT HALL, 1940s. This inviting corner of the great hall in the lodge will beckon a visitor to stop and sit awhile. There are few places better to sit and rest, to converse with friends and family, to read a book, or to watch snow fall on a cold winter's day than the great hall of Starved Rock Lodge.

THE CORRIDOR LEADING TO THE SLEEPING ROOMS, 1940S. The stone flooring of this hallway not only leads to the lodge's sleeping rooms but is also used at the main entrance. Today this hallway leads to the new addition and the indoor pool. Shortly after Starved Rock Lodge was completed in 1939, the the hotel in the lower area was demolished.

A SLEEPING ROOM OF STARVED ROCK LODGE, 1940S. When built, the lodge had 48 rooms and each had knotty pine walls and a private bath. In 1941, the largest Illinois convention of twins, 1,600 individuals, or 800 pairs, convened at Starved Rock State Park, attracting a crowd of 30,000. Many twins stayed in a room much like the one pictured with twin beds.

STARVED ROCK LODGE DINING ROOM, 1940s. A pine-paneled dining room adjoins the great hall at Starved Rock Lodge. In 1939, Starved Rock Lodge advertised a Christmas Day special dinner for $1.25. Regular Sunday dinner was $1. A luncheon menu from December 1950 allows a guest to choose soup, one of nine different entrees, mashed potatoes, buttered wax beans, dessert of pie, cake, or ice cream, and a beverage of coffee, tea, milk, or buttermilk for $3. The $3 price was slashed in May 1951 to $1.40. In September 1955, a similar dinner cost $1.60 with the addition of bottled beer for 35¢. By 1958, a dinner from a similar menu cost $1.75 with the addition of shrimp cocktail for 75¢.

A Statue at Starved Rock Lodge, 1960. This hand-carved statue stands in the great hall of the lodge. In 1935, Sam Sine, or Chief Walks with the Wind, a Winnebago, brought his family to live at the park. He ran an archery range and staged Native American dance programs for visitors. Some 55,000 visitors attended a powwow at Indian Land near the park's west entrance in September 1962 to honor and name the grandson of Chief Walks with the Wind. Over 300 tribesmen from 15 different tribes were represented. Some of dances performed were the green corn and the calumet dances. The green corn dance is performed before the harvest to mark the end of one year and the beginning of a new one. The calumet dance was also performed in 1673 by the Illiniwek in honor of Fr. Jacques Marquette and Louis Joliet. Musical instruments used were a drum (a buckskin-covered pot half full of water), a rattle or a *chichicoya* (a hollow gourd with beads inside), and a flute from hollowed wood. The dancers dramatized a battle between the calumet, or peace pipe, and a hatchet.

Seven

The Legend of Lover's Leap

Standing on Lovers Leap, looking towards
Starved Rock, State Park View,
Starved Rock, Ill.

VIEW FROM THE SUMMIT OF LOVER'S LEAP, 1907–1915. According to legend, a young Illiniwek brave was in love with a Potawatomi maiden. The two lovers were forbidden to marry by their chiefs because of tribal rivalry and taboos against intermarriage. Rather than live without each other, they met one evening at the top of the rock formation just east of Starved Rock, embraced each other, and hurled themselves down to the swirling waters of the Illinois River.

View of Lovers Leap from Mouth of Wild Cat Canyon, midway between Starved Rock and Horse Shoe Canyon, near Ottawa, Utica, La Salle and Peru, Ill.

VIEW OF LOVER'S LEAP FROM THE MOUTH OF WILDCAT CANYON, C. 1907–1915. The Illinois River valley is a haven for wildlife. A great snowy egret may sometimes be found standing on one slender stilt at the river's edge while the other leg remains retracted. At times a great blue heron can be seen standing motionless in the shallow river water feeding on tadpoles, frogs, and fish in the mornings.

Lovers Leap and the beautiful surroundings of Historic Starved Rock, La Salle County, Ill.

LOVER'S LEAP AND THE ILLINOIS RIVER, 1912. From 1905 to 1915, more freshwater fish were harvested from the Illinois River than any other river in the United States except for the Columbia River. Today the Illinois River on either side of Starved Rock is considered to have some of the best sauger fishing in the United States. A fishing tournament is held each spring that attracts many spectators.

Lover's Leap ~ Near Utica, Il[

LOVER'S LEAP AND THE ILLINOIS RIVER, LOOKING EAST FROM STARVED ROCK, 1913. The summit of Lover's Leap is one of several places in Starved Rock State Park where ever-changing beautiful vistas can be viewed. When the sun sets on the Illinois River, it illuminates the pleasure crafts and barges against sandstone bluffs on the water's edge. Endless opportunities for beautiful photographs occur here and throughout the park.

Starved Rock, La Salle Co. Ill.

LOVER'S LEAP, 1913. Many summer resorts have a Maiden's Leap or a Lovers' Rock with similar tales. Usually the legend involves a princess or a maiden that has been jilted or has been forbidden to love or marry. Whatever the reason, they may have leapt to their death below. The woman and sometimes the man will always be remembered as being happier in death than in a life without love.

LOVER'S LEAP LOOKING EAST FROM STARVED ROCK, 1915. A boardwalk runs part of the way on the frequently traveled trail to the top of Lover's Leap. The trail is a fairly easy hike for the less adventuresome. Lover's Leap rises above or is taller than Starved Rock. The summit of Lover's Leap is a great place to look back toward the west at Starved Rock.

EAST END OF LOVER'S LEAP FROM THE ILLINOIS RIVER, C. 1915–1930. It has been said that the Maiden's Leap Rock, more commonly known as Lover's Leap, when viewed from a particular position, looks like a water pitcher. This postcard shows that the profile of Lover's Leap does indeed look like a water pitcher. Also on the card is a couple rowing a boat on the water while idle gentlemen on the riverbank people watch.

LOVER'S LEAP FROM THE ILLINOIS RIVER, C. 1915–1930. At one time, mussels were harvested from the Illinois River. Native Americans used mussels for food and their shells for tools and ornaments. By 1891, mussels provided a major source of supply for the shell button industry. By 1899, mussels became a multimillion-dollar industry. In the early 1900s, parts of the Illinois River were considered the most productive mussel stream per mile in American. A clammer could make about $10 per week (more if he found a pearl) compared to $1 a day for the average laborer in 1899. In 1912, there were 15 button factories on the Illinois River. The pearl button industry died out by the late 1950s when plastics took its place. Today there is a small amount of mussels harvested to provide shells for seed pearl oysters overseas.

LOVER'S LEAP AND THE RIVER FROM THE BIG ELM, C. 1906–1915. Another version of the romantic tale of Lover's Leap has a slightly different twist. An Illiniwek warrior named Belix and a maiden, who was the daughter of Chief Kinebo, the head of the Illiniwek, were to be married. On their wedding day, a great battle began. That battle was the very same battle that led to the Illiniwek seeking refuge on the top of Starved Rock. Belix was killed right before his princess's eyes and fell over the cliff of Lover's Leap to the river below. The distraught princess, knowing she could not live without her love, raised her arms and dove from the cliff to join her love. It has been said that when looking very hard two shadowy figures can be seen on the top Lover's Leap in the misty evening moonlight.

Lover's Leap and Starved Rock, Starved Rock State Park, Illinois

LOVER'S LEAP AND STARVED ROCK, 1948. Yet another legend of Maiden's Leap, or Lover's Leap, goes like this: Wau-Wa-To-Sa was the daughter of an Illiniwek who fell in love with a brave that lingered near her home for months. One day in July, the time came for him to leave. He promised to return in October, but he never returned. Wau-Wa-To-Sa continued to be faithful to her lover, and she continued to wait. Tears sometimes flowed from her eyes. After close to a year, word came that he lived with and loved another maiden. Wau-Wa-To-Sa was very sad and had a very heavy heart. Distraught, she walked to the end of the cliff, sang the death song of her tribe, and plunged into the water below. Her spirit had found peace, and the rocky cliff would forever preserve the tale.

Lovers Leap, Starved Rock State Park, Illinois

LOVER'S LEAP AT EAGLE CLIFF, C. 1930–1945. The Illinois River divides into two channels and is dotted with islands. Bald eagles can be seen resting in trees on several islands, including Plum Island. Plum Island is in the Illinois River directly across from Starved Rock State Park. The island has been purchased by the Illinois Audubon Society to be used as a bird sanctuary. One goal of the Plum Island Sanctuary is to maintain roosting trees needed by the bald eagles that winter there. Approximately 210 species of birds have been identified at Starved Rock State Park. "No matter how I've tried to come up with a more unique location, Starved Rock State Park is undeniably my favorite birding venue," writes John D. McKee, of the Starved Rock Audubon Society. The 45-acre Plum Island Sanctuary has no access and is not open to the public to protect both the wildlife and the Native American archaeological site. Another goal of the society is to replace trees that were removed long ago to allow farming and a small airstrip.

Eight

THE CANYONS

HORSESHOE CANYON, C. 1915–1930. Horseshoe Canyon is formed at the junction of LaSalle and Tonti Canyons. The canyon, located one mile east of Starved Rock, could be reached by following the Native American trail, by excursion boat, or along a path east of the hotel along the river. Horseshoe Canyon begins at the banks of the Illinois River and extends deep into the interior of the park. It was given its name because it winds around and forms a semicircle, or a horseshoe shape. Horseshoes are thought to bring good luck. The luck is contained in the shoe and pours out through the ends. Hanging a horseshoe with the two ends up will bring good luck, but if the horseshoe is hung with the ends pointing down, bad luck will occur.

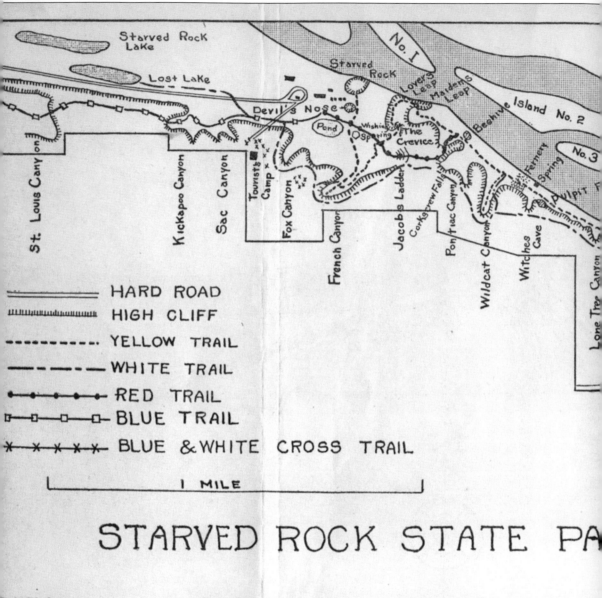

Legend:

─────────── HARD ROAD

ⅢⅢⅢⅢⅢⅢⅢ HIGH CLIFF

– – – – – – – YELLOW TRAIL

— – — – — WHITE TRAIL

●—●—●—●— RED TRAIL

□—□—□—□— BLUE TRAIL

✕—✕—✕—✕— BLUE & WHITE CROSS TRAIL

└─────── 1 MILE ───────┘

STARVED ROCK STATE PA

C. NELSON-

MAP OF STARVED ROCK STATE PARK, 1924. This map is from *Starved Rock through the Centuries* by J. B. McDonnell and Lloyd Eric Reeve. The map shows how Starved Rock State Park looked in 1924. The canyons are much the same today, although the roads and trails are much more developed. Old trails have been blocked off and new trails blazed for the safety of visitors and

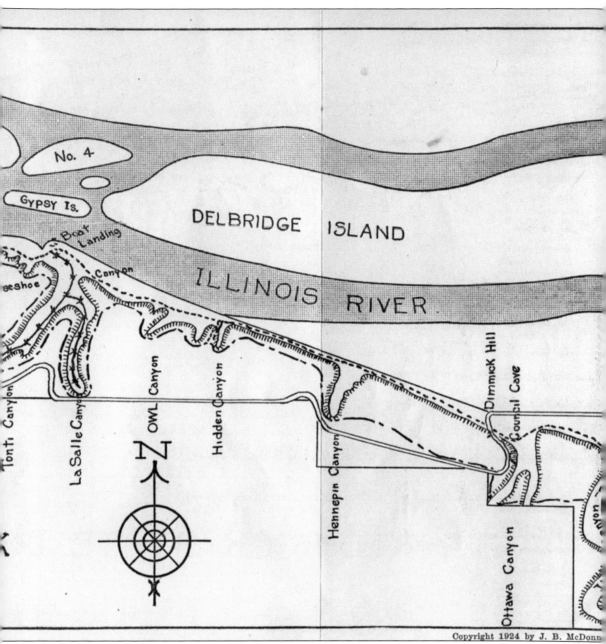

the conservation of the park. The addition of the lock and dam, which had not yet been built at the time of this map, changed how the canyons are accessed. Visitors used to take an excursion boat on the Illinois River to access many of the canyon trails. Today the trails are accessed from the road with parking just a short distance away.

A Gentleman in Horseshoe Canyon, 1907. The gentleman on this postcard is hard to detect next to the massive canyon wall. The deeply eroded canyons are a unique geologic feature to Starved Rock State Park. The canyons today look nearly the same as they would have 4,000 years ago.

The East Branch of Horseshoe Canyon, 1918. Visitors are well aware of the park's outstanding rock formations. St. Peter sandstone was laid down in a huge shallow inland sea more than 425 million years ago and later brought to the surface. This huge up-fold is known as the LaSalle Anticline. St. Peter sandstone lies under much of Illinois but has only a few outcroppings in the state.

THE BROOK AT HORSESHOE CANYON, C. 1915–1930. Hikers can follow this little brook along the trail, as it leads to Horseshoe Falls. Canyons, particularly those at the river's edge like Horseshoe Canyon, offer exciting exploration through heavily wooded terrain and thick underbrush.

HORSESHOE CANYON AT STARVED ROCK, C. 1907–1915. Trails provide enjoyable hikes in Horseshoe Canyon as well as many other areas in the park. Getting in and out of most of the canyons requires moderately strenuous hiking along fairly well-maintained, quiet, and secluded trails. Hiking appeals to all ages and can be done at almost any time of the day or year.

A TRAIL AT HORSESHOE CANYON, C. 1930–1945. The trail pictured goes between the edge of the cliff and the wall of the rock where nature has chiseled large semicircular caves from it. The sandstone wall displays strata of sand colored by mineral deposits in nearly every hue.

MUMMY CANYON, C. 1907–1915. This gentleman has found a great perch from which to throw pebbles into the pond and wait and watch for their rippling effect in the water. Mummy Canyon, located one mile up the Illinois River from Starved Rock, has changed very little since the time of the floods 12,000 years ago. The canyons have very slowly widened and deepened from water runoff.

OTTAWA CANYON, C. 1939–1960. A mother and her child share a quiet moment in Ottawa Canyon, which is located near the east park entrance. The canyon was named for Chief Pontiac's tribe. The Ottawa are members of the Algonquin tribe whose language is Ojibwa. Today the Ottawa populations are mainly located in southern Ontario, northern Michigan, and Oklahoma.

AURORA CANYON, C. 1907–1915. In Roman mythology, Aurora is the goddess of dawn, so the word *aurora* is synonymous with daybreak or dawn. The many colors on the canyon walls appear differently at different times of the day depending upon the amount of light entering the canyon.

ENTRANCE TO AURORA CANYON, 1911. Visitors pose among the shrubs, mosses, vines, and gigantic fern fronds that sprout from the canyons walls. Plants grow on the canyon walls because sandstone is porous and holds water that nourishes the plants' roots. Fifty-nine species of native wild ferns grow in Illinois, and twenty-three species are found in Starved Rock State Park.

POSING FOR A PICTURE IN AURORA CANYON, C. 1907–1915. Scaling the canyon walls must have been difficult for those pictured in this image. Both men and women at this time believed small feet were a sign of good breeding, and they wore shoes a size too small. A lace-up leather boot looked much alike for both men and women, and most owned only one pair of shoes, which lasted for many years.

OSWEGO CANYON, C. 1907–1915. Oswego Canyon was named for the Oswego tribes. The Oswego used the perennial herb bee balm to brew a tea for medicinal purposes. The plant's fragrant citruslike flowers also attract hummingbirds, bees, and butterflies.

FISHBURN CANYON, C. 1907–1915. One theory of how Fishburn Canyon got its name is that the name derives from the Saxon words *fisc*, meaning "fish," and *bourne*, meaning "brook."

93

FISHBURN CAVE IN FISHBURN CANYON, 1910. Outlaws found refuge in the canyons and caves of the park. The hiding place for the "Bandits of the Prairies" was one mile above Horseshoe Canyon in Fishburn Cave. This gang of outlaws was most famous for stealing horses, but it also pursued other crimes such as robbery and even murder.

WATERFALL AND POOL AT THE EAST END OF FISHBURN CANYON, 1908. The gentleman in this image is wearing the latest suit made popular by Edward VII, the Prince of Wales. The prince favored relaxed garments, and these suits became known as the lounge suit or the sack suit. Hard, white tubular collars were worn underneath the jacket as men tried to emulate the image of the "Arrow Shirt Man."

ENTRANCE TO FRENCH CANYON, 1906.
French Canyon was located just east of
the hotel and the cottages that dotted the
ravine between Starved Rock and Lover's
Leap. It was the easiest to reach from the
Starved Rock Hotel.

**A GATHERING OF GENTLEMEN AT THE
ENTRANCE TO FRENCH CANYON,
c. 1907–1915.** This view down into the
canyon puts some perspective on the depth
of French Canyon. Some referred to Starved
Rock as the "Gibraltar of the West" because
of the large rock formations. The odd-shaped
and unevenly weathered canyons and rock
formations were believed by the Native
Americans to be the home of invisible spirits.

French Canyon Starved Rock, La Salle County, Ill.

FRENCH CANYON, C. 1907–1915. Many of the canyons at Starved Rock end in a bowl shape, and large amounts of sand often accumulate on the canyon floors, as shown in this postcard. Notice the erosion, or swales, on the canyon walls. St. Peter sandstone is heavily coated by a "rock varnish." This type of weathering, which produces the uneven erosion to the rock surface, is called differential weathering.

ATWOODS CANYON, C. 1907–1915. This canyon is located one mile above Horseshoe Canyon. Continental glaciers invaded Illinois repeatedly during various ice ages, which occurred from about 2.4 million to 10,000 years ago. The way Starved Rock looks today records the retreat of the last major ice sheet that extended into Illinois from 25,000 to 14,000 years ago.

ILLINOIS CANYON, C. 1930–1945. Illinois Canyon is the largest of all the canyons in the park. It is located a short distance from the east entrance on Highway 71 between Ottawa and LaSalle.

A SCENE IN ILLINOIS CANYON, 1939. A wildflower pilgrimage is held each year so visitors can view and become aware of the abundance and variety of wildflowers growing in the park. Virginia bluebells form a dense carpet along the trails of Illinois Canyon in May.

WILDCAT CANYON, 1907–1915. Wildcat Canyon is located one mile from Starved Rock and just east of Lover's Leap. It could be reached from the hotel by following a path along the Illinois River. The walls of the canyon rise more than 100 feet. Wildcat Canyon is similar to French Canyon except it is much larger and much more impressive.

SITTING HIGH ON A ROCK IN WILDCAT CANYON, C. 1907–1915. Canyons provided relief from the "99 in the shade" temperature as reported in the July 6, 1911, *Ottawa Free Trader.* Throngs of Ottawa residents boarded packed trains headed to Starved Rock, where "people could crawl off in the canyons and timbers and lay down in the grass to pass a day of quiet and rest." Ice cream sales in Ottawa had broken records during the hot spell.

VISITORS IN WILDCAT CANYON, C. 1915–1930. More than likely, the man on this postcard saw deer on his hike. Today deer hunting is allowed in certain areas of the park to help reduce the size of the herds. Herds have depleted many plants. It is felt that it is less damaging to let hunters go off the trails and hunt than to let the herds grow uncontrolled.

KASKASKIA CANYON. The adult pictured is probably pointing out a bird that has come to the water's edge for a drink. Kaskaskia Canyon is located near the east entrance to the park. The canyon was named for one of the Illiniwek tribes.

CLAYTON CANYON, 1912. Clayton Canyon, located one mile south of the Utica bridge, was named for William Clayton, who at one time owned the land where the canyon sets. Bloodroot, a wildflower that grows in the canyons, is one of the first to bloom in the spring at the park. It is an attractive white flower with a yellow center. Although a rather rare plant in most places, it tends to grow on the slopes of the woods in undisturbed areas such as the park. A bright red-orange juice can be extracted from its root or rhizome. This juice was used by Native Americans as body paint and also as a fabric dye. Young men of the Ponca tribe would put the juice on the palm of their hand and then shake the hand of the maiden they wished to marry. Within five days, the juice magically charmed the maiden so she would agree to marry him. This juice should be avoided as it is considered toxic today.

Nine

THE WATERFALLS

THE WATERFALL IN OTTAWA CANYON, C. 1915–1930. The wonderful rock formation of Ottawa Canyon has a large cave and a rippling fall of cascading water. Some of the most scenic waterfalls in the park are found in Ottawa, St. Louis, French, Wildcat, Tonti, LaSalle, Hennepin, Kaskaskia, and Illinois Canyons. This canyon is named for the Ottawa tribe. *Ottawa* means "traders." This tribe became the "French connection" by bringing furs from remote villages to the French for trade. The French in return offered them protection from the invading Iroquois.

LITTLE DEER CANYON, STARVED ROCK, LASALLE COUNTY, ILL.

LITTLE DEER CANYON, 1911. The visitors posing in this image have found one of the 14 waterfalls in the park. Stream-fed canyons gush in the spring and summer and after a heavy rainfall.

FOX CANYON, C. 1915–1930. Fox Canyon was just a short walk east of the boat landing, the hotel, and the parking area. This smaller, deep canyon tended to lure visitors to the larger canyons such as Hennepin or Illinois in hopes of experiencing a much grander site. The canyon was named for the Fox tribes who fought with the Sauk in the Black Hawk War.

HORSESHOE CANYON WATERFALLS,
c. **1907–1915.** This trio poses with arms
extended on the sandstone ledge between the
two waterfalls at Horseshoe Canyon. The
canyon is one of the most beautiful in the
entire park, and the waterfall provides a clear
pool of water at the base.

HIKING IN HORSESHOE CANYON,
c. **1907–1915.** Note the makeshift
ladder extending from the lower level
that this couple climbed to reach their
position. The sight and sound of the
silvery cascade adds the finishing touch
to a hike in to the canyon through the
woods and among the rocks.

Waterfall at Horseshoe Canyon, Starved Rock State Park, Illinois

THE WATERFALL AT HORSESHOE CANYON, C. 1907–1915. The golden age of postcards in the United States was from 1907 to 1915, the same era as the postcard shown. Postcards have been known as souvenir cards because people bought them as a remembrance of their trip. They were also known as a penny postcard because it only cost a penny to mail them.

VISITORS ENJOYING THE WATERFALLS IN HORSESHOE CANYON, C. 1930–1945. Many visitors enjoy the sight and sound of trickling streams that are often torrential in rainy seasons and then drop from the head of the canyon and find their way to the Illinois River.

St. Louis Canyon, 1922. This canyon is named for Fort St. Louis. Excavations done at the site of Fort St. Louis in the 1940s uncovered a bale seal from 1643–1715. Bale seals are an identification tag that was used on textiles. Also uncovered in this excavation was a leather necklace strung with 10 brass Jesuit rings. Many arrowheads, beads, and spoons were also found.

The waterfall in St. Louis Canyon, 1942. On March 14, 1960, three women from Riverside were found murdered in St. Louis Canyon. A lodge dishwasher confessed to robbing and killing the women. A piece of twine from the kitchen of the lodge found on the bodies was a major piece of evidence. He was convicted to life imprisonment and is still serving his sentence at Stateville Penitentiary in Joliet.

WINTER SCENE IN ST. LOUIS CANYON.
St. Louis Canyon is the site of one of the most spectacular ice falls in Starved Rock State Park. Ice falls form in 14 of the 18 canyons when enough moisture falls during fall and winter. The most scenic ice falls are found in St. Louis, French, Wildcat, Tonti, LaSalle, Hennepin, Ottawa, and Kaskaskia Canyons. Ice climbing is allowed in French, Wildcat, LaSalle, and Tonti Canyons.

A FROZEN WATERFALL IN ST. LOUIS CANYON, 1950. St. Louis is a dead-end canyon with walls that soar to 80 feet high on three sides. This canyon is also the farthest west in the park.

106

A WATERFALL IN AURORA CANYON, 1917. Canyon streams during winter temperatures can be stilled with the cold, and sometimes water can be heard gurgling under the ice.

A GENTLEMAN ENJOYING THE FALLS IN FRENCH CANYON, 1908. Some of the longer lasting waterfalls are located in French, LaSalle and St. Louis Canyons. The walls of French Canyon tower to more than 100 feet even though the widest point is only 40 feet. The canyon is 300 feet long. At the far end of the canyon the rocks rise in a series of ledges that resemble stairs, and water cascades down the "stairs."

THE CASCADING FALLS OF FRENCH CANYON, C. 1907–1915. A canyon is a ravine or gorge with higher walls. The word *canyon* is generally used more in the United States, while the word *gorge* is more common in Europe.

THE CANYON WATERFALL IN FRENCH CANYON, C. 1915–1930. Poison ivy, a woody shrub or vine with three leaflets, flourishes in French Canyon as well as many other canyons. The plant can cause a painful, itchy rash. A wise rhyme to remember is "leaves of three, leave them be." Although the plant is a menace to people, birds love eating the greenish-white berries of the plant.

LaSalle Canyon Falls in the East Branch of Horseshoe Canyon, c. 1907–1915. Once reaching the cascading falls at the end of a long hike through the canyon, visitors cannot resist wading in the cool stream.

FALLS IN LA SALLE CANYON, EAST BRANCH OF HORSESHOE CANYON IN STATE PARK, STARVED ROCK, ILL.

LaSalle Canyon Falls, c. 1915–1930. LaSalle Canyon was named for René-Robert Cavelier, Sieur de LaSalle, who was murdered by members of his own party en route to Starved Rock in 1687. He was returning from the coast of Texas, where he had attempted to start a trading station. It is believed that his untimely death had a great impact in the failure of establishing Starved Rock as a permanent military post or French garrison.

THE WATERFALL IN ILLINOIS CANYON. Illinois Canyon is the lower part of Armstrong Creek that was formed when melting glacial waters dug into the area's sandstone about 4,000 years ago. This resulted in the many canyons and ravines along the Illinois River, topped off by the bluff known as Starved Rock, or LeRocher as the French called it.

ANOTHER VIEW OF THE WATERFALL IN ILLINOIS CANYON, 1926. Many trees skirt the edge of the canyon brim. Each spring the bright lilac-colored blooms of the redbud tree are seen scattered throughout the woods. Northern red, black, burr, pin, and white oaks burst with red and yellow colors in the fall at the park. The bark of the black oak is deeply fissured and stands out in the winter months against the snow-covered forest floor.

SAC CANYON, 1926. This canyon is charming and beautiful but small in size compared to Hennepin, Ottawa, or Tonti Canyons. Sac Canyon was named for the Sac, or Sauk, tribes. Black Hawk led this tribe in the Black Hawk War of 1832 against the U.S. government for area land possession. During this war, the two Hall sisters were captured by the Sauk north of Ottawa and then later released unharmed.

THE WATERFALL IN WILDCAT CANYON, C. 1915–1930. One can almost imagine the sound of various birds at the park from this postcard. Wood ducks nest in hollow trees, yellow-bellied sapsuckers drill small holes in cedar trees, scarlet tanagers and cedar waxwings are attracted to serviceberries and northern honeysuckle, red-tailed hawks search for field mice, and nuthatches and chickadees feed on nuts, seeds, and insects.

THE CASCADING FALLS OF WILDCAT CANYON, 1931. A story passed down through the years is that René-Robert Cavelier, Sieur de LaSalle, and Henri de Tonti captured and killed a wildcat in this canyon. Since then it has been known as Wildcat Canyon. Tonti was known as Tonti-of-the-Iron-Hand because he lost his hand in battle. His skillful use of the device his hand was replaced with, or his "iron hand," led Native Americans to believe he possessed special powers.

PONTIAC CANYON, 1916. The canyons are named for the characters of the past. This canyon, of course, is named for Chief Pontiac. Chief Pontiac of the Ottawas fought with the French in defending the Starved Rock area from the English. In the Pontiac Rebellion of 1763, he struggled against the British occupation of the Great Lakes area following the British victory in the French and Indian War.

CURTES CANYON, C. 1907–1915. Just a decade earlier, the people posing in this postcard had probably attended the World's Columbian Exposition in Chicago, where the first postcard in the United States was created to advertise the event. At the fair, they may have seen Buffalo Bill's Wild West Show and been unaware that Buffalo Bill was born just a few miles away from Starved Rock.

CURTES CANYON, STARVED ROCK, LASALLE COUNTY, ILL.

HENNEPIN CANYON. Named for Fr. Louis Hennepin, this canyon and also Tonti Canyon are among the deepest in the park. Hennepin first noticed *charbon de terre*, or coal, along the river in the 1600s. This marked the first discovery of coal in the New World. The Native Americans were fascinated by the "rock that burns" and learned from the French how to forge metal tools with fires fueled by coal.

KASKASKIA CANYON, 1940s. This canyon was named for Kaskaskia, the grand village of the Illiniwek that spread two and a half miles along the northern bank of the Illinois River at Starved Rock. It was the most important village of the Illiniwek from 1673 to 1694. The Iroquois made frequent raids on the Illiniwek, killing their members, burning their villages, and stealing their furs to sell at Fort St. Louis. Although the fort helped to protect the Illiniwek, many eventually moved south and were absorbed by other tribes. About 1750, it was estimated that only about 1,500 Illiniwek remained in the area. During the 1940s and again in the 1970s, archaeological digs were done at the grand village of the Kaskaskia. The site became known as the Zimmerman site as the Zimmermans were the landowners. Little had been known about the Illiniwek before these excavations, but much was gained. Kaskaskia is the only village in Illinois that is definitely identified from the historical records and is associated with a particular tribal group. This study enabled archaeologists to see what native materials were like and the changes that occurred from European contact.

THE FALLS AT THE HEAD OF SALT WELL CANYON, C. 1915–1930. To commemorate William D. Boyce, founder of the Boy Scouts of America, a 16-mile hiking trail was recognized in 1961. The trail begins at the salt well in Starved Rock State Park, heads west to Highway 178, crosses the Illinois River to Utica, then follows the Illinois and Michigan Canal towpath east to Boyce Memorial Drive, and ends at the William D. Boyce grave memorial statue in Ottawa Avenue Cemetery in Ottawa. Boyce got the idea of starting the Boy Scouts of American while on a business trip to London. He had stopped to ask a boy for directions one foggy night, and the boy gave him directions but refused payment. Boyce was so impressed by the boy's "good deed" that he started Boy Scouts of America in 1910.

A TYPICAL CANYON SCENE AT STARVED ROCK, 1934. Those reading the *Ottawa Republican Times* on October 3, 1901, learned of a school trip to Starved Rock to view scenes like the one on this postcard. A special train was run to transport students and teachers of Joliet schools to Starved Rock. It left Joliet at 7:00 a.m. Ottawa superintendents, principals, and teachers were encouraged to join the party at the rock and point out special attractions. Several Chicago teachers were also in attendance, including President Marshall, D. F. Higgins, George M. Campbell, and Conrad Brehm from the school board. Harry Fennimore, master of ceremonies, had a train on hand just large enough for the party, which arrived in Utica in about an hour. Arrangements had been made for a 30¢ fare by buggy from Utica to the rock. A delightful day was had by all.

SCENE AT STARVED ROCK, LASALLE COUNTY, ILL.

A SCENE AT STARVED ROCK, C. 1907–1915. Various trees grow along the roadways, riverbanks, and sandstone bluffs, in the canyons, and throughout Starved Rock State Park. Glaciers thousands of years ago brought seed for red and white cedar trees that grow on the drier sandy bluff tops. Arbor vitae, chokeberry, and mountain holly can be found in the canyons. Papaw, pecan, shagbark hickory, mockernut hickory, black walnut, wild black cherry, hackberry, and Kentucky coffee trees can be found throughout the park. American witch hazel, black huckleberry, wild crab apple, and plum trees skirt the forest edge. The American yew grows on the limestone cliffs and in the canyons. Many white pine trees can also be found in the canyons, some as tall as 60 feet with trunk diameters of 24 inches. The white pine has long blue-green needles that grow in bundles of five and long, large cones. Its wood is soft, light, and durable, and many early buildings in Illinois were built with pine lumber.

TONTI CANYON, 1943. It was believed Henri de Tonti left a large amount of gold near the site of Fort St. Louis, and the mystery of its whereabouts has never been solved. Maybe millions of visitors continue to walk over it each year. Another mystery of where Tonti is buried also continues. Tonti died in 1704 of yellow fever. Some say he was buried with his iron hand at the west side of Fort St. Louis, and others say he was buried near the Mobile River in Alabama. In February 1891, the *Chicago Herald* printed that excavations at Starved Rock had resulted in finding the grave and remains of the famous French commander Tonti. Found alongside the skeleton was Tonti's missing hand. A retraction was made later stating, "The story of the finding of the grave and iron hand of Tonti at Starved Rock, so pompously telegraphed to a Chicago paper, turns out to have been a genuine joke. The people at the Rock know nothing about such a find and laugh at the story as a good joke."

Ten

FURTHER EXPLORATION

307
PULPIT ROCK,
Midway between Starved
Rock and Horse Shoe Canyon,
near Ottawa, Utica,
La Salle, and Peru, Ills.

PULPIT ROCK MIDWAY BETWEEN STARVED ROCK AND HORSESHOE CANYON, C. 1907–1915.
Pulpit Rock is located along the Illinois River midway between Horseshoe Canyon and Starved
Rock. In 1940, Pulpit Rock stood about seven feet high. The pulpit that was formed by nature
is no longer easy to distinguish as it has been worn down by both the elements and visitors over
the years.

ON TOP OF THE PULPIT AT STARVED ROCK, 1914. Two of the ladies in this postcard posed on the top of the pulpit have beautiful large-brimmed hats that extend beyond the breadth of their shoulders to shade the sun from their faces. The ladies may have purchased the hats from Katherine and Nell O'Kane, owners of one of the fine millinery establishments in Ottawa.

DEVIL'S PULPIT, 1909. Pulpit Rock may be the only rock formation that looks different today than when it was first seen by the white men. A reenactment of Fr. Jacques Marquette and Louis Joliet was staged in 1973. Seven men dressed as Frenchmen traveled past Pulpit Rock on the Illinois River to the Mississippi River. Many celebrations were held along the way in various river towns.

DEVIL'S NOSE, 1931. When the Illiniwek sought refuge on the rock, their enemy the Potawatomi showered them with arrows and watched them starve to death from Devil's Nose. Judge John D. Canton of Ottawa addressed the Chicago Historical Society on December 13, 1870, with his speech "The Last of the Illinois and a Sketch of the Pottawatomies." He recounted the legend of Starved Rock, as told to him by Meachelle, the oldest Potawatomi chief.

DEVIL'S NOSE, C. 1939–1960. Devil's Nose is near French Canyon and opposite Starved Rock. It is just one example of the outstanding rock formations in the park. The ridges of the rock are banded and weathered unevenly, creating many fantastic shapes.

STARVED ROCK, 1950. This very creative postcard shows many of the sites to see in Starved Rock State Park. They include Pulpit Rock (S), Devil's Bath Tub (T), Lover's Leap (A), Eagle Cliff (R), St. Louis Canyon (V), Devil's Nose (E), Wildcat Canyon (D), Tonti Canyon (R), the entrance to the lodge (O), falls in LaSalle Canyon (C), and the west entrance (K).

WISHING WELL, C. 1930–1945. From 1912 until 1952, Frank Hart, a member of the Seneca tribe, sold and made beaded rings for park visitors at the wishing well at the far east side of the park. Thousands of visitors tossed coins in the well, and Hart regularly cleaned out the well as another part of his duties. An underground spring runs constantly at this well.

THE *DELTA QUEEN* AT STARVED ROCK, 1973. The *Delta Queen* was a stern paddlewheel overnight steamboat operating on the Mississippi River and its tributaries. It traveled 35,000 miles annually on five major rivers through 16 states and 120 river towns. Other paddleboats on the Illinois River were the *Starved Rock Queen* of the Scenic Boat Company in the 1960s and the *Huron* in the 1890s.

Cave of the Winds, Starved Rock State Park, Illinois

CAVE OF THE WINDS, 1940S. Cave of the Winds is located along the Illinois River just north of Hennepin Canyon. When the wind blows through the cleft of the rock formation, it makes eerie sounds. The Native Americans were afraid that dead spirits lived here, so they avoided this spot.

INTERIOR OF COUNCIL CAVE, C. 1915–1930. Chief Shabbona had a winter hunting camp in and around Council Cave. Council Cave was also a legendary meeting place for tribal councils, and this is how it got its name. It is said that a squaw was chosen to silently sit in on these councils to mentally record the proceedings. This was a position of the highest distinction for a woman.

VIEW OF COUNCIL CAVE. Waterfalls, rivers, and streams have undercut the rock at Council Cave, creating overhangs in the sandstone and forming it into a natural amphitheater.

ARROWHEAD MOTEL. This motel was located a half mile off Route 71 near the entrance to the park. Eight completely modern units adjacent to the lodge and convenient to all points of interests was the motel's advertising pitch.

TURTLE ROCK AS SEEN FROM THE NATIVE AMERICAN TRAIL, C. 1915–1930. Some of the rock formations remind one of prehistoric animals or reptiles.

THE ENGINEERING CORPS, C. 1907–1915. This group of engineers looked the area over and made plans for the future as a resort and a park. The ferry *Princess*, as well as other ferries, was at the hotel landing waiting to take the men across the Illinois River. From there a ride would be waiting to take them to the depot in Utica to board a train for their final destination.

EAGLE CLIFF EAST OF STARVED ROCK, C. 1907–1915. Eagle Cliff is located just east of Starved Rock, Lover's Leap, and the dam along the Illinois River. Eagle Cliff was a favorite nesting place for eagles. Hunters and an increase in visitors greatly depleted the number of eagles at one time until laws were enacted to protect them. Today many eagles can be seen along the river at Starved Rock.

A VIEW OF EAGLE CLIFF, C. 1907–1915. When the river freezes, the once endangered bald eagles find open water to search for fish, which they find in the turbulent waters below the dam. They tend to rest or roost in trees at Leopold and Plum Islands after getting their fill.

EAGLE CLIFF, C. 1915–1930. The highest concentration of eagles is during the coldest time of the year, usually in January. From December through February, generally between 5 to 30 or more eagles at any one time, depending on weather conditions, can be seen. The best place to view the bald eagles is from the top of Starved Rock.

ACROSS AMERICA, PEOPLE ARE DISCOVERING SOMETHING WONDERFUL. *THEIR HERITAGE.*

Arcadia Publishing is the leading local history publisher in the United States. With more than 3,000 titles in print and hundreds of new titles released every year, Arcadia has extensive specialized experience chronicling the history of communities and celebrating America's hidden stories, bringing to life the people, places, and events from the past. To discover the history of other communities across the nation, please visit:

www.arcadiapublishing.com

Customized search tools allow you to find regional history books about the town where you grew up, the cities where your friends and family live, the town where your parents met, or even that retirement spot you've been dreaming about.